# 54

## 3-D Scroll Saw Patterns

# Frank Pozsgai

Schiffer Publishing Ltd

77 Lower Valley Road, Atglen, PA 19310

# Contents

Printed in China.

ISBN: 0-7643-0036-9

Book Design by Michael William Potts.

**Library of Congress Cataloging-in-Publication Data**

Pozsgai, Frank.
   54 3-D scroll saw patterns/by Frank Pozsgai.
     p.  cm.
   ISBN 0-7643-0036-9
   1. Jig saws.  2. Woodwork--Patterns.  I. Title.
TT186.P68  1996
745.51--dc20                     96-9447
                                 CIP

Published by Schiffer Publishing, Ltd.
77 Lower Valley Road
Atglen, PA 19310
Phone: (610) 593-1777
Fax: (610) 593-2002

Please write for a free catalog.
This book may be purchased from the publisher.
Please include $2.95 for shipping.
Try your bookstore first.

We are interested in hearing from
authors with book ideas on related subjects.

# Introduction

If you'd like to improve your scroll sawing abilities, pay close attention! Week after week, as I demonstrate the art of scroll saw cutting, I hear various remarks from those in the audience. It makes me wonder what motivates people to buy scroll saws, considering the lack of self-confidence I hear projected.

Let me share something with you. There is nothing magical or mystical about becoming an expert in the art of scroll saw cutting! A brand-name scroll saw will not automatically make you a better or more proficient woodworker. However, a negative attitude about your own abilities will keep you and anyone who thinks that way from becoming the "pro" one wishes to be.

What will make you that confident expert is believing in yourself. Not only can you do it, but you can do it better than the individual you watched or learned from. The motto for building this self-confidence is simply this:

"practice, practice, and more practice." With experience and patience your abilities and confidence will soar.

One of the things I have enjoyed on the scroll saw is the creation of three-dimensional objects. Over the years I have created many different critters, reindeer to rainbow trout. Now I have reworked my original 3-D patterns and instructions so that fellow band saw enthusiasts can also use them with ease. Carvers, too, will delight in the way 90% of their work is already done before they start!

Enough. So, now that we have established a few positive thoughts, you can stop belittling your abilities and get on to wood cutting. You will see how cutting these 3-dimensional critters will create a conversation piece for years to come. I would appreciate hearing from you about your success with this project, and any suggestions or requests for future pattern designs. Good cuttin' to ya!"

# Instructions & Tips

In creating these 3-dimensional patterns for you, I took into consideration all the governing factors and limitations that would apply to the scroll saw. On some, but not all, patterns, I've added an additional feature of an inside out cut to create a more realistic figure. Geometrically speaking, the rear, front, downward and side views all play a role in developing these patterns.

Band saw users: Read On! Your special instructions are in the next section.

**Instructions for 3-Dimensional
Scroll Saw Cutting**

Cutting these 3-dimensional patterns will certainly challenge even the best scroll saw operator. It truly requires concentration and strength. Remember, it is essential to hold together all your pieces. Since there will be a lot of blade deflection, your best strokes per minute will be 1600 to 1800. Do not overfeed your blade! Allow your cuts to be straight. Indeed your results will be greater per pattern.

**Other Tips**

**1.** On the pattern pages that follow, I've purposely moved each pattern to the left of each page, allowing you to record any notes you may wish to keep for future reference. You may wish to record the type of wood that

seemed to cut best, the blade speed and blade size, or if you had to enlarge or reduce the pattern size due to the cutting capability of your saw.

**2.** Use an Olsen #5, #7, or #9 PGT (Precision Ground Tooth) blades for these patterns. These will allow you to work best in tight radii. The most critical thing to remember about your scroll saw is to make sure you have the proper blade tension. The Rule of Thumb: When you push the blade from front to back with your thumb, you should get a 1/8" deflection. Periodic blade tension adjustment is a MUST. Also, remember to use a tri-square to make sure your blade and saw table are parallel to each other.

**3.** Make several photocopies of each of your masters.

**4.** Precut your wood pieces to the size of the lines of your pattern. Take a photocopy of your pattern and use a gluestick or similar adhesive on the back of the paper, and stick the paper directly to the wood you wish to cut.

**5.** If the selected pattern has an inside cut, drill the smallest hole that will allow the blade to pass through. Proceed to make all the inside cuts first. At this point, you don't have to worry about holding any pieces together. This is the reason you make inside cuts first with each pattern.

**6.** After the inside cuts, always proceed to cut the 3/4" edge first, making sure you hold the pieces together as you cut. After finishing this, turn your pattern face up and make all the necessary cuts.

**7.** Separate your pieces and out pops your finished product! If, for some reason, you wish to retain all of the pieces, place the pattern all together and use either Scotch-tape or clear box tape on the top and bottom to hold it together. Then place a rubber band around it to contain it. (This is in the event that you wish to show it off to your friends. Hey, why not? You did it!!)

Good luck, and have fun with these patterns. Ask your dealer about more of our 3-dimensional patterns, which will be a follow-up to this introductory book.

### Tips for Band Saw Users

Bandsaw users can simply enlarge the existing paper patterns. You can take them to a maximum/optimum working height of 4" to 5", with a 2" thickness and 12" length. Use a 1/16" band saw blade to perform these cuts, but never rush your cut. Take your time!

Just remember these three simple steps:

**1.** Make all inside cuts first, on the scroll saw, through the 2" thickness.

**2.** Raise your fence on the band saw to just about 1/4" above the height of your material. Watch your hands and fingers! Hand and finger position are critical in making these cuts, and also to your safety. It would be a good idea to purchase and review my 3-dimensional Scroll Saw Cutting Techniques and Projects videotape. Essentially, the cutting techniques you'd learn would apply to the scroll saw. Now, start by making your top cut first. The right side first and then the left, always holding you pieces firmly together.

**3.** Now turn the pieces once more, back to the 2"-thick side, and proceed to cut the silhouette on your scroll saw.

### Choosing Wood
*Cutting Only on the Scroll Saw (Unfinished):*
Pine, Alder, etc.
*Carving, Scroll Saw & Band Saw:*
Bass Wood, Tupelo, Jelutong, Sugar pine

### Carving Tip
Each carver has his or her own style, but ruby tipped rotary bits, such as flame, medium or small ball type bits are excellent. They are designed to run up to 35,000 rpm maximum.

### Painting Tip
Use acrylic paint in the liquid form. Krylon's 1301 Clear finish works well.

# Cuttin' a Coho Salmon

The secret of good three dimensional scroll saw work is having the wood perfectly square. Be sure of this before gluing the pattern to the wood.

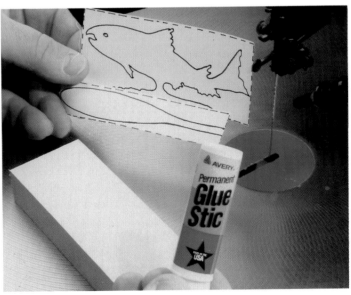

Use a common glue stick to apply the pattern to the block. A spray adhesive will also work.

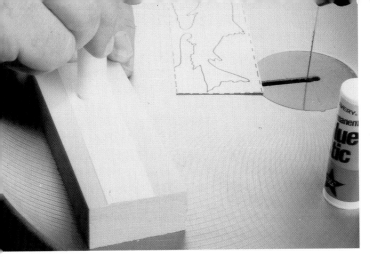

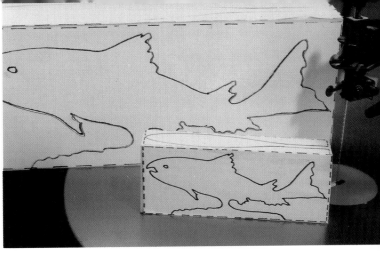

Apply a generous amount of glue to the back of the pattern...

The patterns may be enlarged to any size, while using the same techniques. The only limit is the clearance of the scroll saw arm. If a bandsaw is available, you may use it to cut the top view.

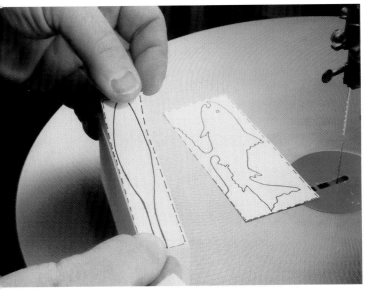

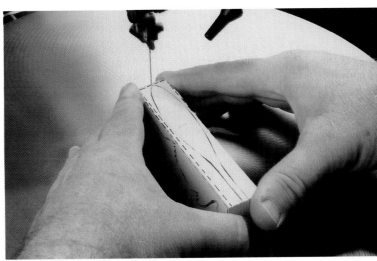

and press it in place.

Cut the top view first. You must clear away anything on the saw that will limit your maneuverability. This may include the blade guard and hold down. You will also want to move the air nozzle out of the way. You always want to have your hands low enough so they won't be pinched by the arm.

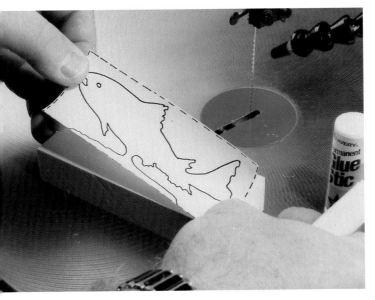

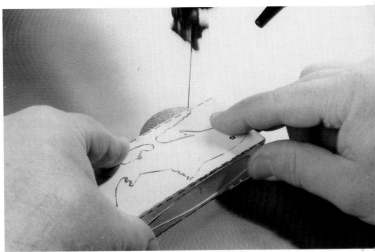

Do the same with the profile pattern, making sure it faces in the correct direction.

Next cut the profile.

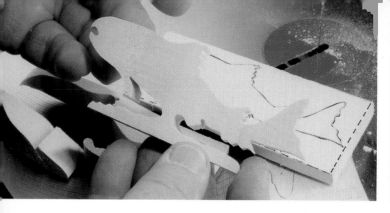

The result.

Work with finer rotary tools or traditional carving tools to create the details.

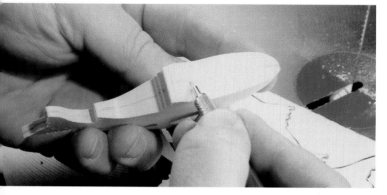

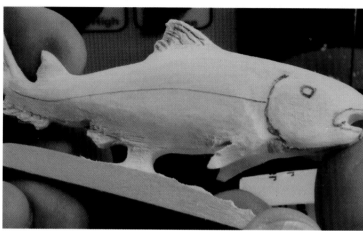

Draw a center line down the top of the fish.

Sand with 220 grit paper, and the fish is ready for finishing.

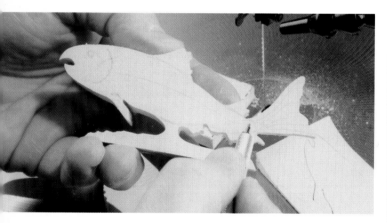

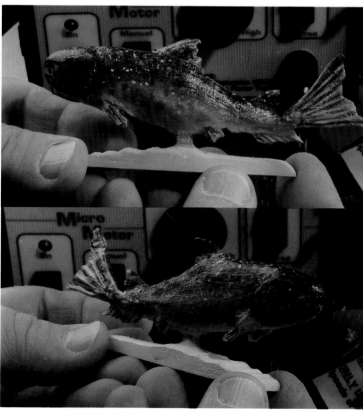

Mark the details of the fish.

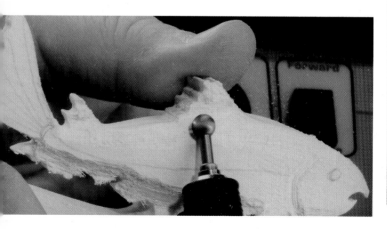

A rotary carving tool can be used to set the basic shape.

I have chosen to paint this fish. A natural finish can also be used, but the woods should be chosen accordingly.

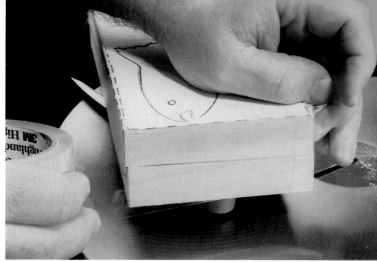

Taping the ends after completing the top cut keeps things together while you cut the profile.

As said earlier the top view cut of the larger fish requires the deeper throat of the bandsaw.

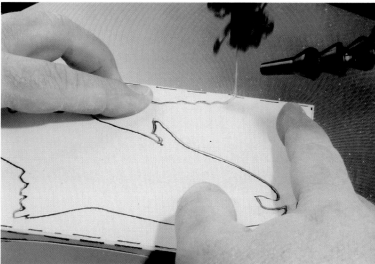

When the top view is done you can return to the scroll saw for the profile cut.

The result.

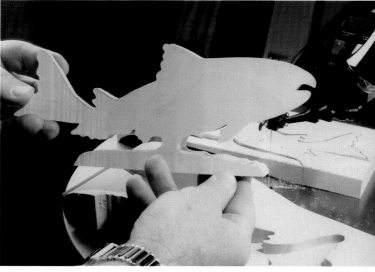

The result. It can be finished in the same way as the smaller version.

# The Gallery

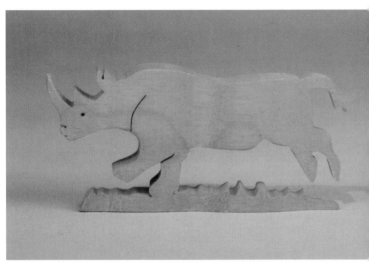

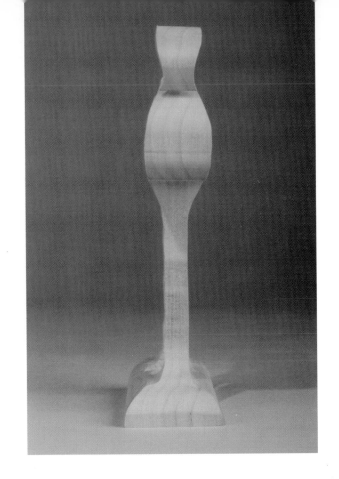

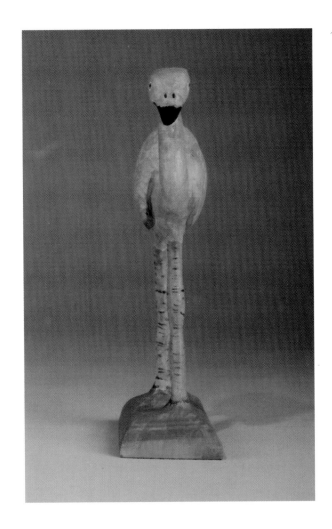

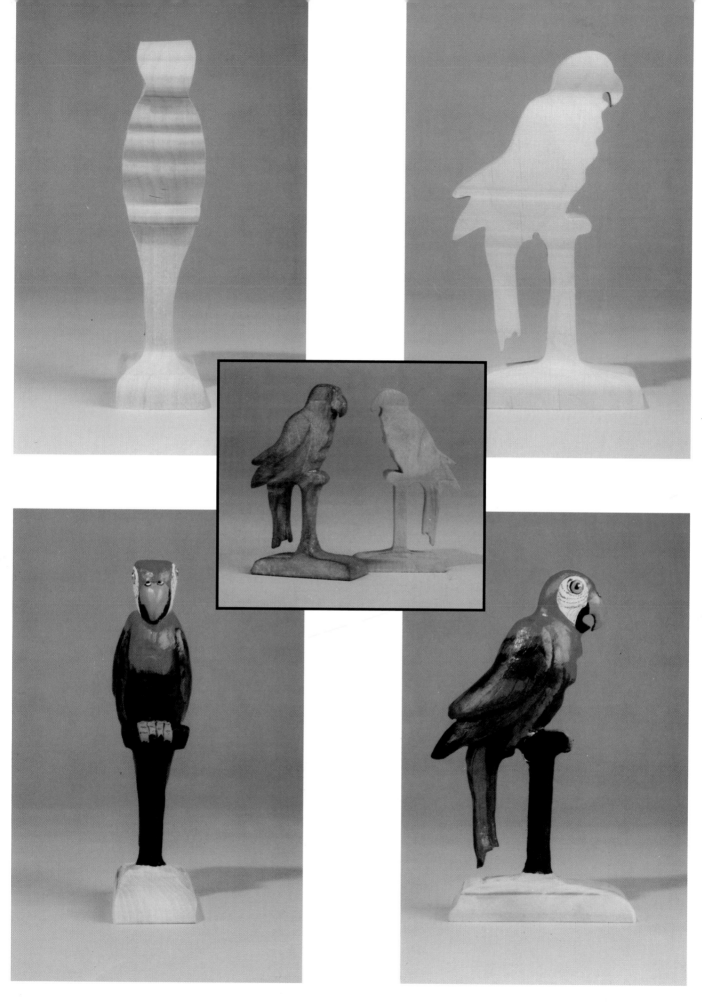

12

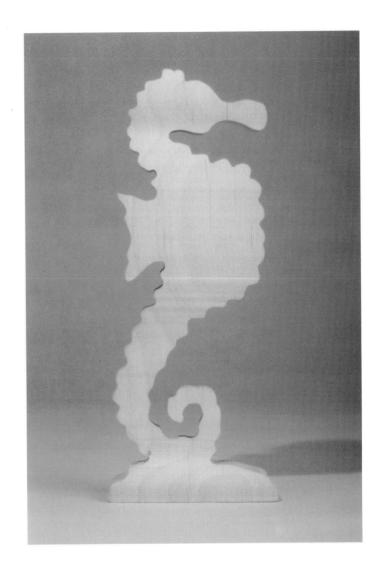

13

14

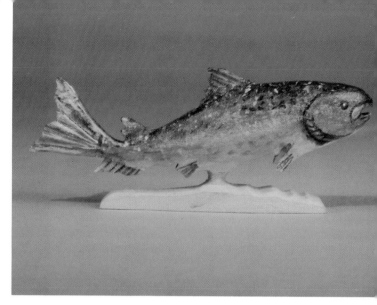

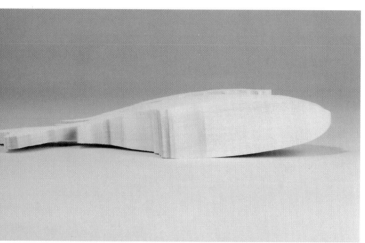

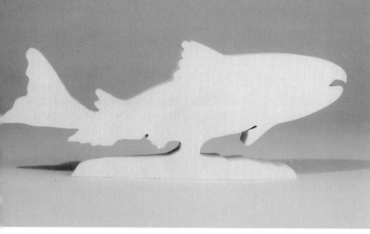

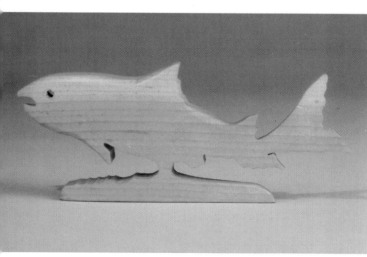

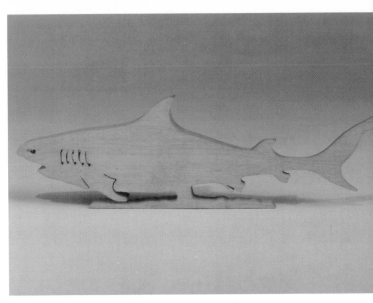

# Typical 3-Dimensional Paste-up and Sequential Cutting Steps for Two-sided, 3-D Cuts

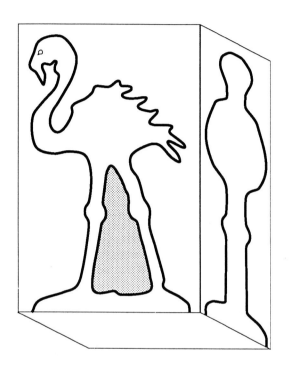

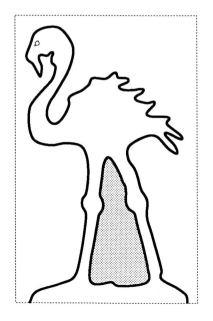

**The Flamingo**

Step 1. After making several copies of your master pattern, cut along the dotted line and use a glue stick to paste the pattern to each side. Always do all the inside cuts first. Drill a 1/8" hole between the bird's legs and pass through your blade and make this cut.

Step 2. Start the second cut on the 3/4" edge, first on one side, then the other, holding the pieces together. Do not overfeed the saw. Maintain a steady, gentle pressure.

Step 3. Now, turn your piece on its side and make this cut. Note: always cut clockwise. Start at the front edge of the bird's leg. Take your time. These cuts are demanding on your hands.

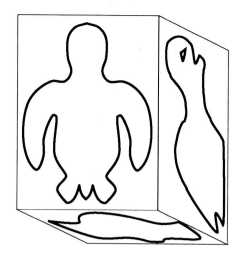

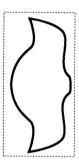

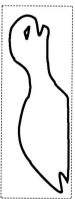

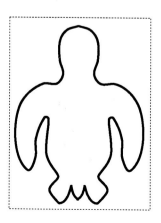

## The Turtle

Step 1. After making several copies of your master pattern, cut along the dotted line and use a glue stick to paste the pattern to each side.

Step 2. Start your first cut with the 2" piece of wood on edge. First do one side (the front view), then the other (the side view). Do not overfeed your saw, simply maintain a steady, gentle pressure.

Step 3. Turn you piece on its side, holding all parts together, and proceed to cut this pattern. If you wish, you can use some Scotch tape to help hold every thing together firmly.

Step 4. Once again, turn your piece on its face side and make this cut. Always cut clockwise. Start at the left rear flipper. Take you time. These cuts are demanding on your hands.

# Patterns

## Land Animals

### Golden Retriever

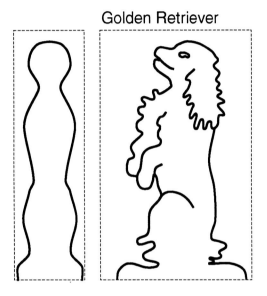

### Kitty Cat

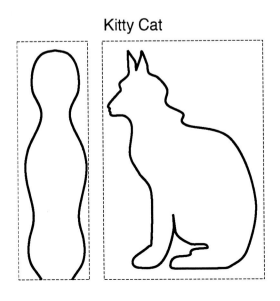

## Scottish Terrier

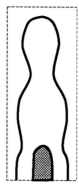

## Malamute Husky

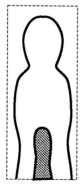

## Golden Retriever

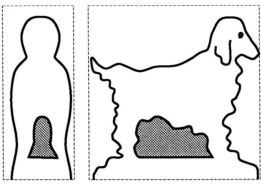

## Poodle

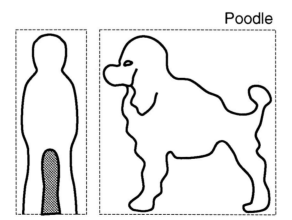

## Springer Spaniel

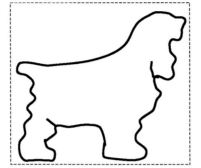 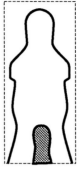

## Australian Shepherd

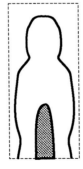 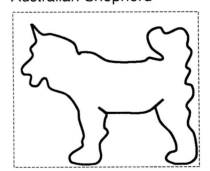

Rhino

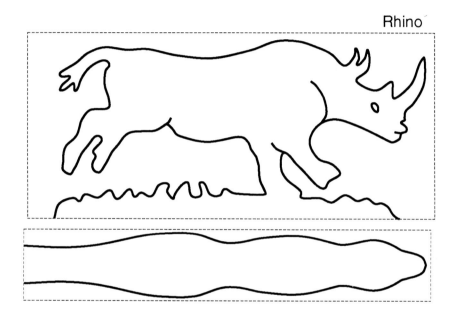

**Bear**

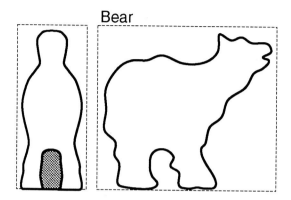

**Squirrel**

Kangaroo

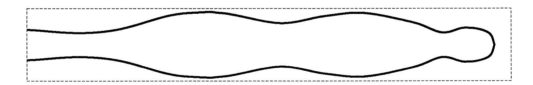

Giraffe

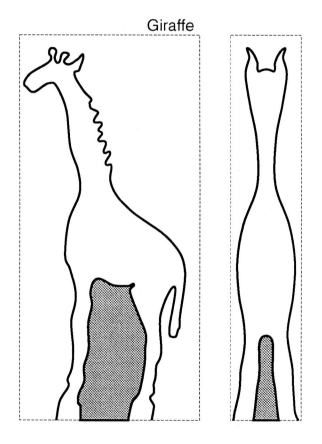

Moose

 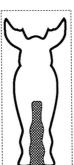

Llama

Raccoon

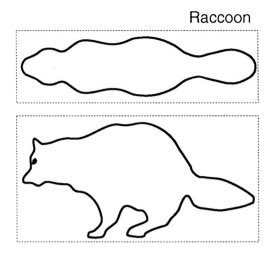

River Otter

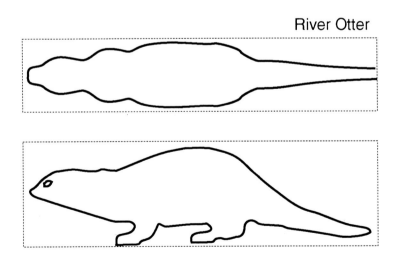

Goat

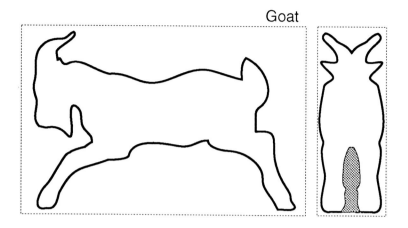

Horse

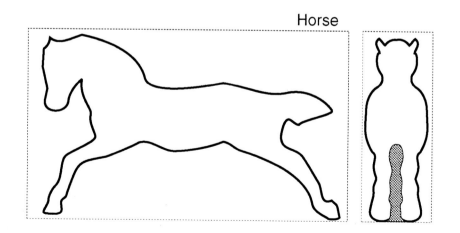

Rabbit

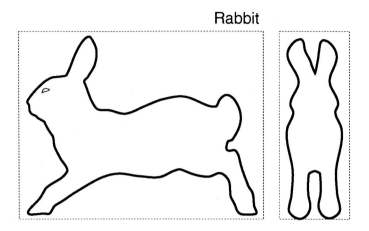

Skunk

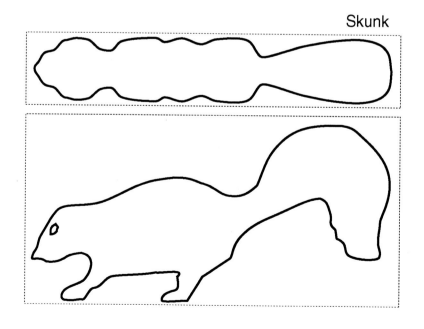

# Flying Things

Pelican

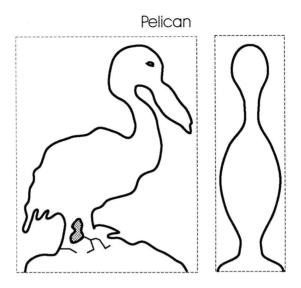

Parrot

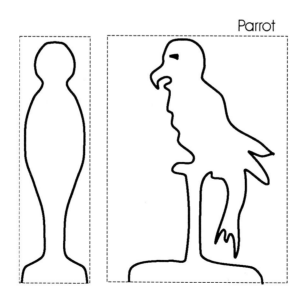

31

Gull

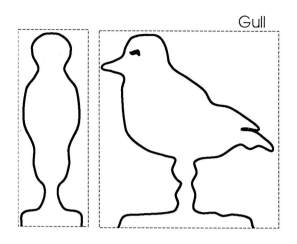

Quail

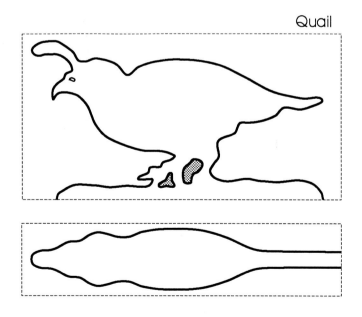

## Parrot

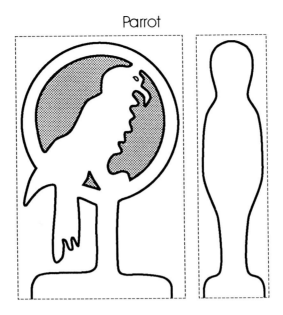

## Cardinal

## Eagle

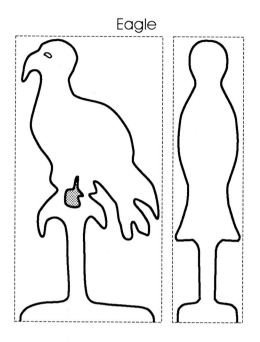

## Vulture

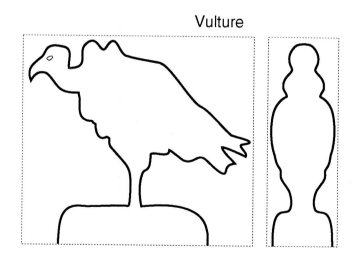

Duck

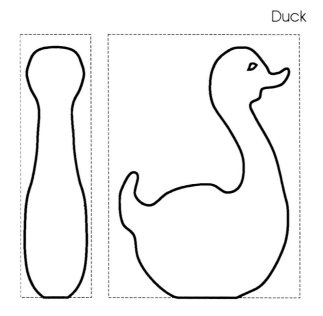

Goose

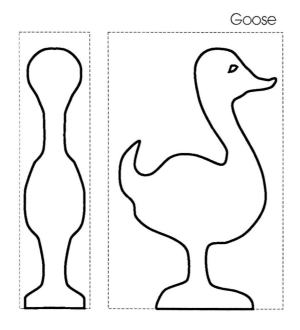

Swan

Duck

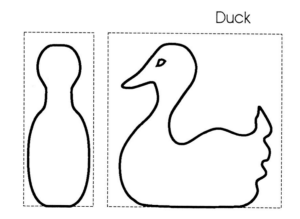

Chicken

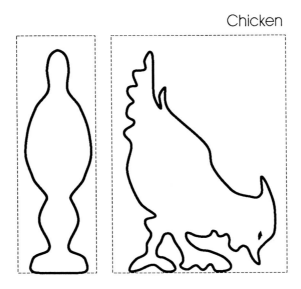

Ostrich

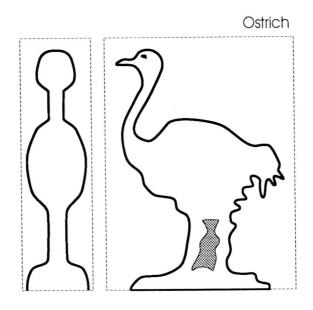

Turkey

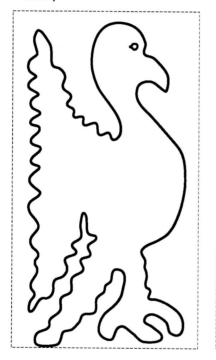 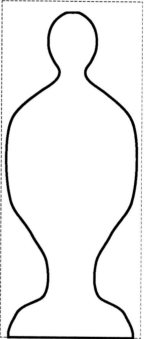

**The turkey is designed
to be made
from thicker stock.**

## Great Blue Heron

## Flamingo

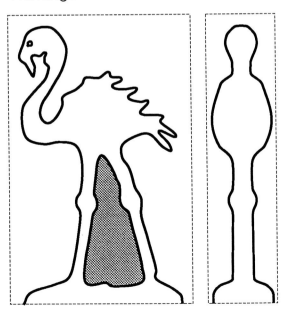

Sparrow

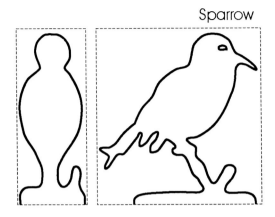

Pigeon

# Watery Creatures

Angelfish

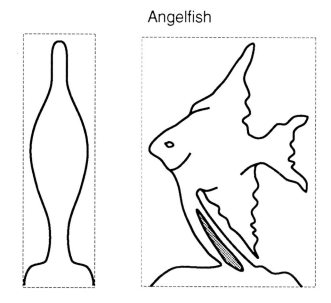

Swordfish

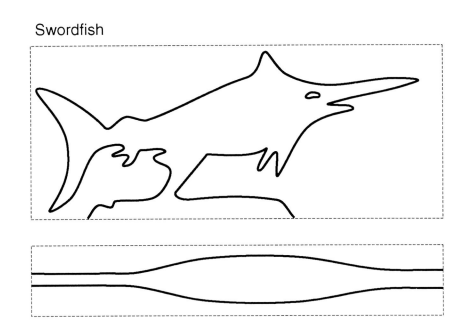

## Bottle-Nosed Dolphin

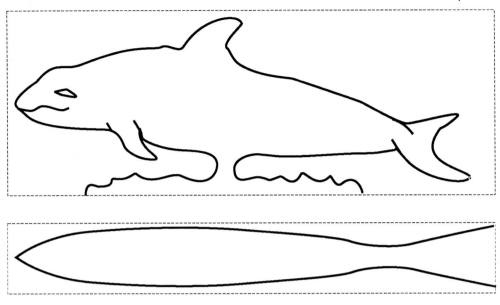

## Tuna

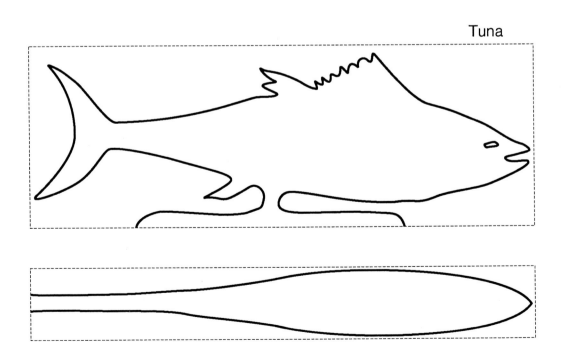